SMART NATION

SMART NATION

Published by Smart Nation

smartnationhq.com

Copyright © 2024 by Smart Nation

ISBN 979-8-9920238-1-7 (paperback)
ISBN 979-8-9920238-0-0 (ebook)

A blueprint for the future.

♥ ⬠ ● ◆ ★

For the People of the
United States of America.

TABLE OF CONTENTS

♥ ⬠ ● ◆ ★

PREFACE

Hello!

If you're reading this book, it's probably because you're not satisfied with life as it is, and you're seeking a new direction. You've come to the right place. *Smart Nation* is a blueprint for a better way of life for us all.

Harnessing the power of automation technologies, we aim to build a fairer, more sustainable tomorrow: a future where you can always pursue your passions and achieve your American Dream, no matter your background or circumstances.

First, we'll guarantee you receive the five things you need to live in the modern age: care, housing, income, education, and freedom (or CHIEF for short).

Second, we'll cut your taxes: zero taxes for people making under $250,000 each year.

Finally, to pay for it all, we'll create new companies owned by *you*. Every dollar in profit will fund your benefits.

We're building a movement to inspire and empower the world to dream again.

Welcome to the Revolution.

- Smart Nation

PREFACIO

¡Hola!

Si estás leyendo este libro, probablemente sea porque no estás satisfecho con la vida tal como es y estás buscando una nueva dirección. Has venido al lugar correcto. *Smart Nation (Nación Inteligente)* es un plan para una mejor calidad de vida para todos nosotros.

Aprovechando el poder de las tecnologías de automatización, nuestro objetivo es construir un mañana más justo y sostenible: un futuro en el que siempre puedas perseguir tus pasiones y alcanzar el Sueño Americano, sin importar tus antecedentes o circunstancias.

Primero, te garantizaremos que recibas las cinco cosas que necesitas para vivir en la era moderna: asistencia médica, vivienda, ingresos, educación y libertad.

Segundo, reduciremos tus impuestos: no impuestos para las personas que ganan menos de $250,000 cada año.

Finalmente, para pagar todo esto, crearemos nuevas empresas de tu propiedad. Cada dólar de ganancia financiará tus beneficios.

Estamos construyendo un movimiento para inspirar y empoderar al mundo para que vuelva a soñar.

Bienvenidos a la Revolución.

– Smart Nation

CHAPTER ONE:
INTRODUCTION

The Revolution begins with you.

You may not be into politics. You may not be a voter. You may not even be much of a reader. But you're critical to building our future, so thank you for being here.

In this book, we'll identify the sources of our problems, propose new solutions, and share a vision for the year 2050 and beyond.

Our plan is to recruit an army of revolutionaries – Americans of all backgrounds – to rebuild our nation from the ground up.

This book is just a starting point. With your input, details of the Smart Nation plan will change time and time again, but our core mission – to enable your American Dream – will remain constant.

First, a bit of history.

As far as we know, we humans started as tribes in Africa. These tribes developed simple tools.

Over generations, we spread to other areas of the world, and our tools became increasingly advanced – from the invention of stone tools to the use of early metals to the construction of sophisticated automation systems, such as machines powered by wind or flowing water.

We built equipment to farm more efficiently and to industrialize. We invented electronics, including the telephone and the computer.

And more recently, we created the internet to connect the world.

Wherever there was a need, humans developed a solution. In short, human evolution was driven by our ability to create ever more advanced tools.

Today, we live in a global civilization with sophisticated technology and complex systems. Our businesses are increasingly automated with artificial intelligence and robotics, leading to higher efficiency and greater output.

Our tools have become so powerful that we're quickly reaching a level of automation that will allow us to sustain ourselves with minimal human labor.

Just think: soon computers and robots will handle everything – from building homes to manufacturing clothing to producing and delivering food.

What if these technologies could work for *you*?

In the age of automation – when we'll experience a boost in economic productivity and output unlike anything we've seen before – you deserve to live for free.

That's why we'll guarantee you receive the five things you need to live in the modern age: care, housing, income, education, and freedom (CHIEF).

Care
Comprehensive healthcare so you can live well.

Housing
A place of your own so you can feel safe.

Income
Money to pay for food and essentials.

Education
Knowledge and skills to pursue your passions.

Freedom
Security to choose your own path.

These rights not only protect your ability to live but also represent an investment in our shared future.

That is, we believe that if your basic needs are met, you'll pursue your passions and go on to do great things that will benefit us all.

But that's not all.

We also have a planet to take care of. You can't be free and happy if you're living in a world of environmental disasters.

Experts tell us we can stop climate change and save Earth by reducing our carbon footprint, which means we must redesign our economy to be sustainable end-to-end: from sourcing to production to distribution to consumption to waste management and resource regeneration.

So how do we simultaneously guarantee your new benefits and create a sustainable economy?

Smart Nation is the solution.

If we want to build a better future, we need to change course. And to do so, we need a new strategy.

That's why the Smart Nation plan proposes a comprehensive set of solutions to 1) upgrade and democratize our economy, and 2) simplify and modernize our government.

First, we'll redesign our economy.

Today, we have an economy consisting of mostly privately-owned businesses. These businesses sell goods and services to consumers and each other.

Our new economy will include companies owned by the public – but independent of government – that will compete alongside privately owned businesses. These companies will be for-profit and built for sustainability.

They will operate in almost every industry and serve all cities and states. This new confederation of public-owned companies will be called USA Enterprises.

USA Enterprises will fund and deliver your new benefits.

Second, we'll reorganize our government.

We'll restructure the Senate and Cabinet to be focused on four main areas: 1) human capital, 2) resources and infrastructure, 3) economy and education, and 4) international affairs.

We'll also scale back the government's role. With USA Enterprises offering guaranteed healthcare, housing, income, and education to all, we'll eventually be able to phase out most government-run welfare programs.

And as we eliminate programs and reduce the budget, we'll cut your taxes: zero taxes for people making under $250,000 annually.

To further empower states, cities, and private companies, we'll cut unnecessary federal regulations. This will result in a lean federal government.

With a redesigned economy and reorganized government, we'll be better positioned to achieve our vision of freedom and opportunity for all.

In the coming chapters, we'll discuss how we'll specifically improve the five key components of modern civilization: 1) human capital, 2) resources and infrastructure, 3) economy and education, 4) international affairs, and 5) organization and governance.

- **Human Capital:** Investing in people as our greatest asset, with a focus on care, housing, income, education, and freedom.

- **Resources & Infrastructure:** Upgrading our energy systems, food production, water distribution, raw materials acquisition, construction, transportation, city services, and urban development.

- **Economy & Education:** Redesigning the economy and preparing our people for the jobs of the future, with an emphasis on creativity and entrepreneurship.

- **International Affairs:** Prioritizing economic collaboration, human rights protections, conflict de-escalation, and multilateral nuclear disarmament.

- **Organization & Governance:** Restructuring the government for efficiency and effectiveness.

The time for change is now.

Automation will drive never-before-seen efficiencies in a faster-than-ever timeframe, creating an economy of abundance.

We can either embrace this change and leverage it to our collective benefit, or suffer the painful consequences of inaction with worsening economic inequality and environmental destruction.

You are the change we need. Join us on this journey to continue the American experiment and build a new nation, together.

♥ ⌂ ● ◆ ★

CHAPTER TWO:
HUMAN CAPITAL

If you were to grow a garden, you'd need to plant seeds. And for those seeds to germinate and grow, you'd need to give them water, nutrients, air, light, space to grow, and protection from pests.

It's a basic formula for success. Provide those necessities, and your garden will flourish. Fail to do so, and you'll have a lot of dead and languishing plants.

Humanity is no different. To achieve our collective potential, we must invest in our people. We must invest in *you*.

So to help you be your best, we'll guarantee you receive the five essentials to life in the modern age: care, housing, income, education, and freedom (CHIEF).

♥ ⌂ ● ◆ ★

CARE **HOUSING** **INCOME**

EDUCATION **FREEDOM**

- **Care:** Universal, comprehensive healthcare (alongside private options), including preventative care, physical care, mental care, rehabilitative care, urgent care, and specialized care for children, seniors, and people with disabilities.

- **Housing:** Affordable housing for all who want it with a free option for those in need.

- **Income:** Basic income to pay for necessities, such as food, personal care products, clothing, and household items.

- **Education:** Free education and training from early childhood development to PreK-12 through university and beyond,

preparing individuals for the jobs of the future.

- **Freedom:** Ensured protection of human rights.

We'll especially protect your right to individual liberties – from your freedom of speech to your freedom of worship to your freedom of love – no matter your race, gender, age, religion, beliefs, sexual orientation, or gender identity.

Self-Defense

When it comes to gun rights and regulation, our country can't agree on nationwide policy.

You have the right to protect yourself, your loved ones, and your community. You also deserve to live in a place with the gun laws you want.

Rural areas and cities have very different needs. That's why we're for empowering states and cities to determine their own gun legislation.

Under the Smart Nation plan, the Constitution will federally protect the right to self-defense, but not gun ownership.

Instead, individual states and cities will set gun policy in their respective territories. By localizing gun laws, we'll be better able to cater to the values and preferences of each community.

However, we'll continue to apply federal restrictions and ban civilians nationwide from owning destructive devices, as defined by the National Firearms Act.

To improve gun safety, we'll encourage the use of new technologies, such as personalized smart guns that require user authentication to activate.

It's also worth noting that to reduce violence in all its forms, we must address the root causes of the problem, including socioeconomic inequality, gang conflict, and mental illness. We'll tackle these challenges by offering universal economic benefits, implementing community-based violence intervention and education programs, and providing free mental healthcare services.

Criminal Justice

No matter the circumstances, everyone deserves to live a life that's free from torture.

We'll advocate for comprehensive reform of our criminal justice system, focusing on crime prevention and rehabilitation.

Privacy

We'll explicitly guarantee your right to privacy in the Constitution.

Marijuana Legalization

In line with your right to privacy, we'll legalize marijuana nationwide.

Body Autonomy

While abortion is a complicated issue, we recognize that it's a personal decision, and we'll protect everyone's right to control their own body.

More specifically, a pregnant person should have the federally protected right to choose to abort a pregnancy up to the 24th week of gestation, or later in some cases for medical reasons.

Additionally, we must reduce the need to choose by providing:

- **Unwanted pregnancy prevention:** Offer a variety of free contraceptives.

- **Child support:** Make it easier to raise a child (particularly for single parents) with universal healthcare, housing, income, education, and childcare.

- **Adoption and foster care options, and public boarding schools:** Provide more support within the adoption and foster care systems and create new public boarding schools that offer children a safe, healthy, and enjoyable childhood experience.

Mind Autonomy

With upcoming technological advancements, we'll need new safeguards to protect our mental independence.

We'll incorporate the right to freedom of thought into the Constitution.

CHAPTER THREE:
RESOURCES & INFRASTRUCTURE

At this pivotal moment in our country's evolution, we have an opportunity to modernize our infrastructure and redesign our business practices around energy efficiency, climate resilience, resource renewal, and environmental sustainability.

We'll pursue sustainable resource acquisition and infrastructure development through USA Enterprises (our new, public-owned companies). In doing so, we aim to facilitate the adoption of eco-friendly practices by the rest of the private sector.

♥ ⌂ ● ◆ ★

Our approach consists of three parts:

- **Procure resources ethically.**
  USA Enterprises will ethically source and distribute our resources, such as food, water, and raw materials.

  We'll ensure our supply chain operates in a manner that protects the environment. We'll also prioritize sourcing from local and regional suppliers to reduce our carbon footprint and support local economies.

- **Harness clean energy.**
  To facilitate our country's transition to clean energy, USA Enterprises will invest in new energy systems.

  We'll harness renewable energy sources (such as solar, wind, wave, and geothermal), and develop new conversion, storage, and distribution infrastructure.

We'll also pursue the discovery of new energy sources and technologies that allow us to drive down the cost of clean energy.

In the near term, as we move away from carbon-emitting fuel sources, we'll invest in secure nuclear power plants to meet our growing energy demand while generating minimal carbon emissions.

- **Build sustainable infrastructure.** USA Enterprises will develop energy-efficient and environment-friendly technology, materials, buildings, and practices.

We'll repair, upgrade, create, and maintain America's infrastructure, including transit systems, irrigation systems, and other public works projects.

Food Production

To feed our people, we'll need to grow more food. USA Enterprises will invest in traditional farmland and new vertical farms, and we'll use automation technologies to produce crops efficiently and inexpensively.

We'll phase out the practice of factory farming and create a more compassionate and sustainable food system by switching to free-range and cultivated meat and dairy.

Water Distribution

Everyone deserves clean water. USA Enterprises will develop new water distribution infrastructure to provide safe and reliable drinking water to all.

Raw Materials Acquisition

When it comes to the acquisition of raw materials, such as mining and forestry, USA Enterprises will purchase existing companies so

that you own some of the means of production alongside private enterprise.

Construction
We're going to be building a lot. USA Enterprises will create electric-powered, autonomous heavy equipment and robotics to facilitate end-to-end construction.

And we'll automate the entire construction process to increase efficiency, improve safety, and reduce costs and construction time.

Transportation
In the first phase of USA Enterprises' infrastructure plan, we'll develop a transcontinental thoroughfare with a high-speed railway and autonomous vehicle superhighway.

It'll connect the country's two largest cities – New York and Los Angeles – and run through the geographic center of the U.S. mainland, linking

Cleveland, Chicago, Omaha, Denver, and Las Vegas.

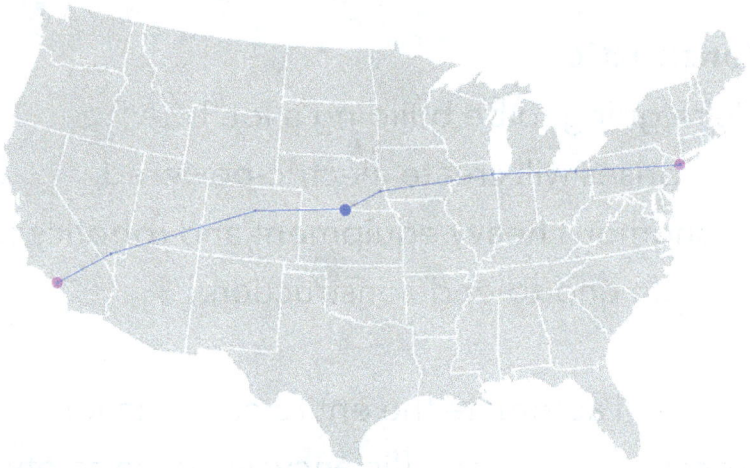

By 2050, this new transportation system will include many other routes that will collectively connect most cities by high-speed transit.

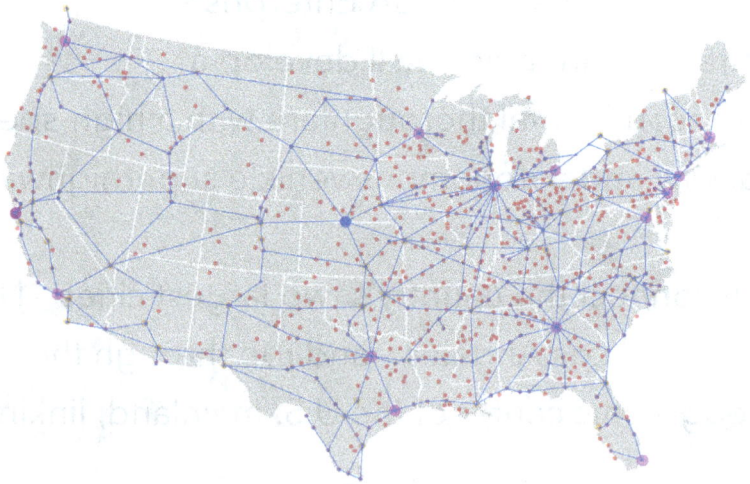

USA Enterprises will also develop new air and sea infrastructure to enable all modes of transportation.

City Services

USA Enterprises will provide upgraded city infrastructure and services, such as subways, street cleaning, and waste management.

We'll also develop climate-resilient infrastructure to protect our cities from natural disasters.

Urban Development

USA Enterprises will develop entirely new cities consisting of residential areas, parks and playgrounds, schools, care centers, hotels, shopping districts, entertainment and cultural venues, recreation facilities, commercial spaces, and public transportation systems.

These new urban centers will be located adjacent to existing cities as well as in undeveloped areas. They'll feature high-density

housing surrounded by abundant green space, offering a mix of city and country living.

CHAPTER FOUR:
ECONOMY & EDUCATION

The United States economy is large, complex, and highly productive. Due to present-day automation technologies, such as artificial intelligence and robotics, it's becoming increasingly efficient.

But it's structured to enrich a privileged few at the expense of the many and prioritize short-term corporate profits over the long-term survival of our planet.

As a result, we face two overlapping challenges: economic unfairness and environmental destruction.

First, our economy is not fair.

For many Americans, it feels harder than ever to find work and make ends meet. And it's only

going to get worse because our jobs as we know them are going away.

Automation has already begun to displace all kinds of jobs. Self-checkout kiosks are replacing cashiers, chatbots are replacing customer service representatives, robots are replacing factory workers, and algorithms are replacing financial traders.

And it's only a matter of time before self-driving vehicles replace truck and taxi drivers, computer-generated images replace actors and models, and artificial intelligence software replaces lawyers and accountants.

According to some experts, by 2050, computers and machines could replace more than half of the activities people are paid to do today. Absent significant changes, we're facing an unprecedented economic crisis, where very few of us prosper wildly and too many of us are left with nothing.

Second, our economy is not sustainable.

Because of bad practices such as the use of fossil fuels, we're slowly destroying our environment.

Caused by human-generated carbon emissions, climate change is now a global crisis. Shifting weather patterns and their associated impacts pose an existential risk to humanity, increasingly threatening public health and safety, economic prosperity, and international stability.

Without an immediate change in direction to reduce our carbon footprint, global warming will lead to more natural disasters, food shortages, new disease outbreaks, and social unrest.

We have a better way.

USA Enterprises, an independent set of companies owned by the People, will create a new public-sector economy built upon fairness

and sustainability, with a focus on driving innovation, productivity, and job growth.

Its purpose will be to serve the common good.

As a corporation (completely separate from the government), it will compete in the private sector alongside private enterprise.

To attract the best and brightest minds to work for USA Enterprises, compensation will be based on merit and comparable to what employees would earn in the rest of the private sector.

Because cities are home to nearly 90% of the United States population (according to the University of Michigan Center for Sustainable Systems) and the main source of carbon emissions, our economic plan focuses on urban and suburban areas.

Working across all U.S. cities, we aim to achieve four key objectives:

- Develop renewable energy sources, sustainable practices, and new infrastructure.

- Ignite innovation, grow new industries, and create high-quality products and services.

- Generate profit and distribute income and benefits to the public.

- Prepare our people for future jobs and create abundant job opportunities.

So how will it all work?

The USA Enterprises plan has two parts:

- **Currency:** A digital currency, Americoin.

- **Companies:** A group of for-profit companies, USA Enterprises.

Americoin

Americoin

A digital currency designed for security, simplicity, and flexibility, Americoin will support the USA Enterprises ecosystem of products and services with financial infrastructure.

The Americoin Blockchain will be a secure, scalable, and reliable blockchain that will serve as the technological backbone for Americoin.

Americoin will serve four purposes:

- **Medium of exchange:** Each coin will be usable as a payment method at USA Enterprises.

- **Store of value:** Each purchased coin will be pegged to the U.S. dollar and interest-bearing, like a savings account.

- **Funding mechanism:** Capital raised from the sale of coins will fund our initial launch as well as ongoing development and infrastructure projects.

- **Distribution vehicle for universal basic income:** Limited-use coins will pay for food and essentials.

AmericoinX

Every United States citizen will receive a weekly income in the form of AmericoinX.

Unlike Americoin, AmericoinX will not be interest-bearing. It'll also be limited to food and essentials and expire at the end of each week.

USA ENTERPRISES

USA Enterprises

We'll create a group of seven companies – USA Labs, USA Markets, USA Studios, USA Works, USA Care, USA Homes, and USA Talent – that will collectively offer a public option for almost everything.

Our companies will work together to address our environmental and economic challenges and ensure that the fruits of labor automation are produced sustainably and distributed fairly.

LABS   **MARKETS**   **STUDIOS**

WORKS   **CARE**   **HOMES**   **TALENT**

USA Labs

USA Labs will be the technology, research, and development arm of USA Enterprises. It'll pioneer and commercialize new tools and technologies, including electronics, digital media, communications and information systems, transportation systems, and smart city infrastructure.

USA Labs will also be responsible for developing the Americoin Blockchain and Americoin.

USA+ will serve as a universal digital identity and portal to the USA Enterprises ecosystem of products, services, utilities, and applications. It'll include, among other things, a search engine, social network, email and communications platform, productivity suite, digital wallet, creator content platform, TV streaming service, music and podcast streaming service, mapping and navigation service, and personal assistant.

USA Research will be responsible for research and development in emerging technology areas. It'll seed the innovation pipeline with new intellectual property and facilitate productization across economic sectors in areas such as artificial intelligence, drones and robotics, renewable energy, life sciences, sustainable materials, electronics, quantum computing, cybersecurity, immersive technologies, neural interfaces, high-speed transit, and space and sea technologies.

USA Markets

USA Markets will sell and deliver all goods and services, including food and grocery items, electronics, clothing, shoes, jewelry, beauty and health products, home goods, gardening tools, office supplies, toys, pet supplies, sporting goods, automotive and other vehicles, and travel.

USA Markets will include an online market that you'll access through USA+. As a marketplace

for everything, it will sell whatever brands you want to buy, including your favorite existing brands, as well as products and services under our own brands.

USA Markets will also consist of offline commerce with physical shops, grocery stores, restaurants, hotels, and entertainment and recreation venues.

Our delivery service, USA Go, will ensure fast, inexpensive, and reliable delivery of goods and packages.

Through USA Markets, creators – such as product developers, fashion designers, and chefs – will be able to participate in profit-sharing. This arrangement will provide entrepreneurs with a substantial financial incentive directly tied to the success of their creations.

USA Studios

USA Studios will produce and showcase art, culture, and entertainment, including photography, design, fine art, architecture, dance, theater, movies, television, music, podcasts, books, magazines, games, augmented and virtual reality, sports, esports, events, museums, science centers, location-based entertainment, and theme parks.

As with USA Markets, USA Studios will offer profit-sharing with creators, such as artists, musicians, writers, and performers.

USA Heritage will promote and preserve American culture and traditions.

Through USA Studios, we'll empower the creator community and usher in a global creative renaissance.

USA Works

USA Works will be the resources and infrastructure arm of USA Enterprises, with a mandate to develop and maintain all public works projects in and between cities.

It'll be responsible for the planning and execution of our 25-year, $25 trillion infrastructure program, through which we'll repair, upgrade, create, and maintain America's infrastructure.

USA Real Estate will purchase land and acquire raw materials, including existing agriculture, mining, and forestry companies.

USA Nature will be responsible for restoring and preserving our natural ecosystems.

USA Energy will construct new solar, wind, wave, geothermal, and nuclear energy systems, and a smart electric grid. It'll also assist USA Labs in

the discovery and commercialization of new energy sources.

USA Ways will develop, manage, and maintain tunnels, bridges, railways, highways, and stations. This transit system will be designed for safety, reliability, and speed. By 2050, it'll enable high-speed intercity commutes for over 80% of the United States population.

Additionally, USA Ways will build and maintain other transportation infrastructure, including ports, airports, vertiports, and a nationwide network of electric vehicle charging stations.

USA Rides, accessible through USA+, will offer a point-to-point transit service using driverless vehicles and eVTOL (electric vertical take-off and landing) aircraft.

USA Works will upgrade and subsidize existing city infrastructure and services, such as public transit, internet, water, waste management,

street cleaning, snow plowing, and emergency response.

It'll also create entirely new cities, such as CityAmerica: a smart megacity built from the ground up at the heart of the United States mainland.

USA Space will develop new infrastructure, including nationwide spaceports, to support the emerging space industry.

USA Care

Offering free, comprehensive healthcare and rehabilitation services, USA Care will be responsible for all care activities within USA Enterprises.

Leveraging new technologies, it'll provide high-quality, personalized healthcare, including USA Health for physical care, USA Well for mental care, USA Vision for eye care, USA Dental for

dental care, USA Hospitals for urgent care, and USA Life for rehabilitative care.

USA Care Centers, like your local doctor's office, will provide primary and specialty care services. And they'll offer specialized care for children, seniors, and people with disabilities.

USA Life Centers will provide rehabilitation facilities and services.

USA Care will encourage preventative care, offering good nutrition through USA Foods (our grocery stores) and a variety of exercise options through USA Fit (our fitness initiative).

USA Seniors, our senior care program, will address all the needs of our aging population – from meal delivery to socialization – so they can lead happy and healthy lives, and continue contributing to society.

Under USA Access, we'll provide special accommodations for seniors and people with disabilities, including free ride services.

USA Care will also offer fee-based offerings, such as premium services, cosmetic procedures, and veterinary care.

USA Homes

USA Homes will create and manage smart home communities, offering luxury and affordable housing units, and a free option for those in need.

We'll build housing campuses within existing cities as well as entirely new cities. They will feature integrated amenities, including parks and playgrounds, co-working and commercial spaces, shops and restaurants, cultural and entertainment venues, recreation facilities, and protection, safety, and wellness services.

This integrated approach aims to create self-contained communities with convenient access to essential services, workspaces, and recreational opportunities.

To further enhance the overall living experience, USA Homes will integrate new artificial intelligence and robotic technologies that will automate in-home services, such as cooking, cleaning, and maintenance.

USA Talent

Responsible for education and training, USA Talent will offer end-to-end education services – including early childhood development, PreK-12, university, vocational training, and ongoing learning – and it'll facilitate open access to information, technology, and skills training programs.

With online and in-person courses, USA Talent will focus on preparing our people for the jobs of the future. It'll offer five development tracks in

the areas of food, entertainment, technology, care, and home (collectively the FETCH economy).

From elementary to middle to high school, USA Schools will incorporate vocational training and be equipped with state-of-the-art technology, collaborative workspaces, and creative studios. In cultivating creativity and ingenuity at an early age, we'll ensure that the next generation of workers is competent to contribute to the future economy.

Additionally, USA University will offer advanced studies and job training for people of all ages.

USA Kids will be a comprehensive childcare program, providing a safe, nurturing, and educational environment for children throughout the year.

USA Play will integrate play-based learning activities into public spaces and community programming.

USA Caregivers will give parents and guardians additional support and resources to create more effective at-home learning environments.

Similar to public libraries, USA Learning Centers will feature public educational tools and resources, such as 3D printers and virtual reality simulators.

For adults seeking to hone their skills, USA Training will facilitate real-world learning opportunities, internships, and apprenticeships within the USA Enterprises portfolio of companies.

Local Enterprises

While many products and services will bear the USA Enterprises brand, each city will have its own branded companies, such as NYC Enterprises and LA Enterprises, catering to local needs.

NYC LA

Board of Directors

Like any other corporation, USA Enterprises will be governed by a Board of Directors. The USA Enterprises Board will be elected by USA Enterprises employees.

The Board will be responsible for hiring key executives, coordinating activities, and setting the long-term strategic direction of the confederation.

It'll consist of 30 individuals from diverse backgrounds who are considered leaders and visionaries in their respective fields.

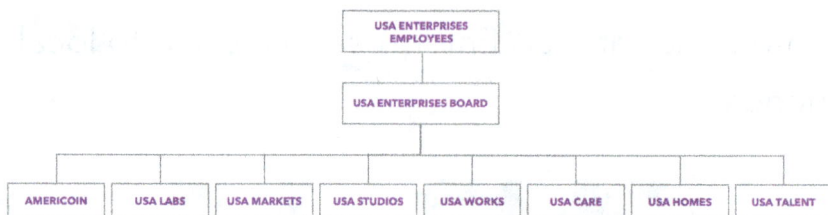

```
                    ┌──────────────────────┐
                    │   USA ENTERPRISES    │
                    │     EMPLOYEES        │
                    └──────────┬───────────┘
                    ┌──────────┴───────────┐
                    │ USA ENTERPRISES BOARD│
                    └──────────┬───────────┘
  ┌────────┬────────┬──────────┼──────────┬────────┬────────┬────────┐
┌────────┐┌────────┐┌────────┐┌────────┐┌────────┐┌────────┐┌────────┐┌────────┐
│AMERICOIN││USA LABS││USA     ││USA     ││USA     ││USA CARE││USA     ││USA     │
│         ││        ││MARKETS ││STUDIOS ││WORKS   ││        ││HOMES   ││TALENT  │
└────────┘└────────┘└────────┘└────────┘└────────┘└────────┘└────────┘└────────┘
```

CHAPTER FIVE:
INTERNATIONAL AFFAIRS

We live in an interconnected, global community. So no matter how much we improve our country, we won't ever achieve the full potential of humanity if our fellow nations and peoples aren't thriving as well.

That's why we're for international cooperation and collaboration.

Our foreign policy will be anchored by a set of global objectives that capture the ultimate goal of our worldwide civilization and a shared vision for humanity:

- **Propagate humanity:** It's our biological reason for being. We'll encourage reproduction to continue and expand our species, and we must reinvest in and preserve our environment to sustain ourselves and future generations.

- **Achieve contentment:** Every human deserves to live a life of mental and physical well-being. We aim to support each individual with care, housing, income, education, and freedom.

- **Acquire knowledge:** We seek to expand our tools, skills, and knowledge base through research, innovation, discovery, and transfer.

- **Advance our understanding**: We're on a quest to uncover truths – however revolutionary or controversial – about life, the universe, and overall existence.

If we can all agree on a common mission, we'll be better able to reconcile our differences and collaboratively pursue the same end goals.

♥ ⬠ ● ◆ ★

But, despite our pursuit of global harmony, we are a nation with geographic boundaries, and we must secure our borders.

Secure Borders

We'll end unauthorized immigration. We can't have people here unvetted and undocumented.

Using drones, cameras, sensors, and artificial intelligence, we'll create a virtual border wall. All trespassers will be banned from entering the country.

Extraterritorial Border Cities

To accommodate migrants and refugees seeking asylum, we'll build new cities at the border – extraterritorial border cities – that will abide by our laws, but not be part of the United States.

These cities will provide all the resources and infrastructure needed to sustain a high quality of

life for all residents while they go through the immigration process.

Easy Immigration
We have a moral obligation to serve as a haven for anyone, anywhere in the world who seeks freedom and opportunity. Plus, we'll need population growth beyond new births to accelerate the expansion of our economy.

We'll welcome vetted individuals who wish to move to the United States with a fair and seamless immigration process.

Citizenship
Nobody deserves to live in the shadows, no matter how they got here. And we can't have people in our country who are undocumented.

That's why we're for naturalizing all immigrants. We'll create an immediate pathway to citizenship – with proper vetting for criminal

history – for our 11 million undocumented immigrants.

Smart Cities

INTERNATIONAL

Smart Cities International

Through Smart Cities International, a global alliance, we'll make our technology available to other nations and territories to reconfigure their own economies around fairness and sustainability.

Smart Cities International will help create locally-managed enterprises that offer citizens healthcare, housing, income, and education, and facilitate the transition to a sustainable economy.

Through this alliance, we'll also advocate for other nations to respect and protect individual liberties.

Free and Fair Trade

Global economic collaboration means an open exchange of ideas, goods, and services.

We'll embrace free and fair trade policies and bilaterally reduce tariffs to the greatest degree possible.

Open Space

Space exploration, research, and development should be approached on a global and collaborative basis.

SpaceCo

We'll ensure space is an international territory and military-free domain by creating an international space coalition, SpaceCo, to govern space exploration, development, settlement, and security.

Mars and Beyond

Consistent with our mission to propagate humanity, we aim to become an interplanetary species. We'll settle on Mars and establish a footprint on a second planet.

Our international coalition, SpaceCo, will be responsible for coordinating the settlement of Mars. This settlement will establish its own society and system of governance, based on

democratic principles and subject to international law.

Security and Defense

Despite our desire to collaborate with other nations, our country faces serious threats. We'll protect America and our allies from those who seek to harm us and destroy our way of life.

To do so, we'll fund and develop new defense infrastructure, leveraging artificial intelligence, drones and robotics, cybersecurity, advanced weapons, and other emerging technologies to equip our military with superior capabilities in a fast-evolving landscape.

But nobody benefits from warfare, particularly nuclear warfare. And we're focused on achieving long-term, sustainable peace. So we'll also seek to de-escalate conflicts around the world and pursue multilateral nuclear disarmament efforts.

Artificial Intelligence Containment Treaty

Artificial intelligence offers immense potential to revolutionize industries, enhance human lives, and solve complex global challenges, but it also presents significant risks and dangers.

We'll seek to make an Artificial Intelligence Containment Treaty with our allies and adversaries to regulate artificial intelligence research, development, and deployment, and in doing so, ensure the safety and security of our worldwide community.

CHAPTER SIX:
ORGANIZATION & GOVERNANCE

Born in 1776, our nation is nearing its 250th anniversary. While our Constitution has endured, we have progressed well beyond the imaginations of our founders.

Over the past couple of centuries, our federal government has ballooned in size and taken on functions better served by the private sector. As a result, our taxes have gone up as well.

In addition, though our civilization has grown monumentally more complex from where we began, our representatives in Congress are still expected to have comprehensive knowledge of all issues and be well-versed across the spectrum of stakeholder needs.

This has resulted in many elected officials without the proper background and knowledge to legislate effectively for all constituents.

We have a better way.

We'll advocate for a separation of the economy and government: a free market system with minimal government regulation or interaction.

We'll also reduce the size of our government. Using artificial intelligence, we'll automate administrative functions and make government operations more efficient.

And with USA Enterprises offering guaranteed healthcare, housing, income, and education to all, we'll eventually be able to phase out most government-run welfare programs, from the Supplemental Nutrition Assistance Program (SNAP) to Medicare and Medicaid.

As we reduce the budget, we'll cut your taxes: zero taxes for people making under $250,000 annually.

We'll also reorganize our government to be more effective.

Here's how it'll work:

Just like our current government, our new government will have three branches: legislative, executive, and judicial.

Legislative

The legislative branch, Congress, will be responsible for passing laws and amending the Constitution. It'll consist of two houses: the House of Representatives and the Senate.

As it is today, the House of Representatives will consist of members elected to represent geographic areas. Each district will have one

representative, popularly elected by the people within that district.

But we'll restructure the Senate. Instead of state-based representation (two Senators per state, regardless of size or population), we'll have age-based and issue-specific representation.

Three Senators will be elected on a national basis by each of four age groups (17-29, 30-49, 50-69, 70+) for each of four focus areas (human capital, resources and infrastructure, economy and education, and international affairs), for a total of 48 Senators.

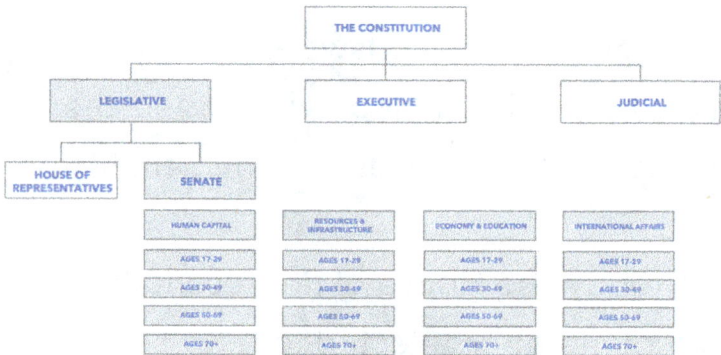

Executive

The executive branch will include a President and Vice President who will be popularly elected nationally, without an electoral college.

We'll restructure the Cabinet to include six primary members: Secretary of Human Capital, Secretary of Resources and Infrastructure, Secretary of Economy and Education, Secretary of Homeland Security, Secretary of State, and Secretary of Defense.

The Human Capital Division will consist of the Departments of 1) Housing and Urban Development, 2) Health and Human Services, 3) Veteran Affairs, and 4) Justice.

The Resources and Infrastructure Division will oversee the Departments of 1) Food and Agriculture, 2) Energy and Climate, 3) the Interior, and 4) Transportation.

The Economy and Education Division will lead the Departments of 1) Commerce, 2) the Treasury, 3) Labor and Automation, and 4) Education.

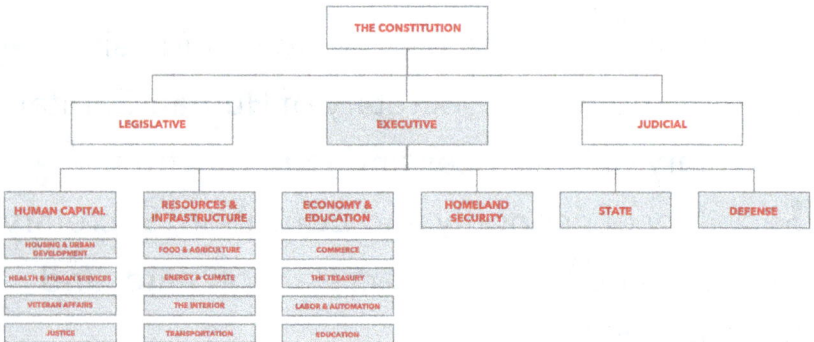

Judicial

The third branch, the Judiciary, will be responsible for interpreting and reviewing laws.

To incorporate more diverse perspectives on the Supreme Court and mitigate extremism and polarization, we'll support the expansion of the Court to 13 justices (nine of which are already in place today). To implement this plan, one new justice will be appointed in the first year of each of four consecutive presidential terms.

By expanding the Court, we'll also protect the separation of powers between the branches, as it becomes less likely that any ill-intentioned President will be able to nominate enough justices to control the Court.

Instead of the indefinite tenure that Supreme Court justices hold today, we propose implementing a term limit of 20 years.

States and City-States

Cities have very different needs from rural areas. We aim to empower individual communities to self-govern on a localized basis.

To that end, we believe that cities should be able to choose independence from their states to become city-states. Under the Smart Nation plan, any city with a population greater than 100,000 may opt to join the United States as an independent city-state.

For congressional districting purposes, each city-state will continue to be considered part of its host state, but all other government functions will be separate.

Puerto Rico & Washington, D.C. Statehood

If approved by a majority of Puerto Rico's residents, we'll seek to grant statehood to Puerto Rico, offering fair representation in our federal government. With 3.2 million residents, Puerto Rico would be the 32nd largest state in the United States.

We'll also make Washington, D.C. a city-state.

And as other U.S. territories grow in population, they too will be eligible for statehood.

Taxes & Regulation

With the elimination of government-run welfare programs and automation of government services, we'll reduce our expenses.

As a result, we'll be able to cut your taxes, beginning with zero taxes for anyone earning under $250,000 annually.

We'll purge outdated laws and deregulate industry wherever possible. For instance, we'll legalize marijuana, end minimum wage, and eliminate mandatory corporate benefits, such as the employer health insurance mandate.

Where necessary, we'll implement new regulatory frameworks to guide and coordinate the expansion of emerging industries and technology sectors, such as artificial intelligence, robotics, neural interfaces, cryptocurrency, and virtual reality. In doing so, we'll protect your rights, ensure your safety, facilitate healthy economic activity, and drive sustainable growth.

National Debt

In the long term, USA Enterprises will generate enough profit not only to pay for our benefits but also to help repay our debts.

First, we'll reduce the budget and stop borrowing money while USA Enterprises covers the cost of new social programs, infrastructure, and urban development.

Second, we'll supplement tax revenue to help pay off the outstanding debt. We aim to be a debt-free nation by 2100.

Free and Fair Elections

A free and fair election system will have the best results. To avoid big money influence, we must remove the need for fundraising, which means we must eliminate the need for funds.

To do so, we'll:

- Change our election laws and cut out administrative hurdles that necessitate excessive campaign spending.

- Remove the cost of campaigning by developing a public media platform and

digital forum, thereby offering all candidates equal opportunity to share their plans and communicate directly with voters.

Public HQ

Public HQ will be a centralized online hub for civic engagement. It'll focus exclusively on engaging voters in meaningful discourse around issues and policies.

Campaign Tools

Aiming to level the playing field for first-time and outsider candidates, we'll make it easier for anyone to launch a campaign and show public support.

For instance, we'll offer a turnkey "campaign-in-a-box" subscription service to break down the barriers to running for office, and we'll develop a real-time, people-powered poll to quantify and demonstrate all candidates' traction, irrespective of political affiliation.

Voting Rights

We'll seek to extend the right to vote to 17-year-olds and expand civics education to ensure they're properly informed.

Election Day

To make it easier for you to vote, we'll make Election Day a federal holiday.

Digital Government

USAGov will be your portal to our government and will include everything you need to access and engage with our departments and agencies, as well as track our progress and performance.

It'll include a virtual assistant to help navigate our government, answer any of your government-related questions, and receive your feedback.

News Media

Corporate media is inherently biased toward corporate interests.

USA News will fund free, comprehensive, real-time, independent news coverage from citizen journalists to ensure you know the truth about what's happening in the world around you.

National Mission Statement

Despite our differences, we're one nation – defined by a shared set of values and a common mission.

That's why we'll memorialize our collective objectives in a national mission statement:

to enable freedom, opportunity, and justice for all.

Constitutional Convention

To make some of our proposed changes, we'll need to rewrite the United States Constitution. 2026, the 250th anniversary of our nation's founding, is an opportune moment for us to begin that process.

First, we'll update pronouns, remove outdated references, and integrate amendments into the main body of the text.

Second, we'll incorporate city-states, restructure the Senate and Cabinet, and enshrine your rights, including:

- Your right to protect yourself, your loved ones, and your community.

- Your right to privacy.

- Your right to control your own body and mind.

A constitutional convention requires approval by two-thirds of both Houses or two-thirds of the state legislatures, so we'll need to build a coalition of supporters in Congress and state legislatures across the country.

CHAPTER SEVEN:
CITYAMERICA & CITYPLEX

To galvanize our country, we need a national call to action: a generational project of unprecedented scope and scale.

That's where CityAmerica comes in.

CityAmerica

CityAmerica

CityAmerica will be our nation's new economic capital. With 12 million residents, it will be one of the largest cities in North America.

As a model metropolis of the future, CityAmerica will be built from scratch with new smart city technologies and infrastructure.

Located at the geographic center of the U.S. mainland at the Kansas-Nebraska border, it will be the central hub of our next-generation transit system, USA Ways, linking most cities with a network of high-speed railways and autonomous vehicle superhighways by 2050.

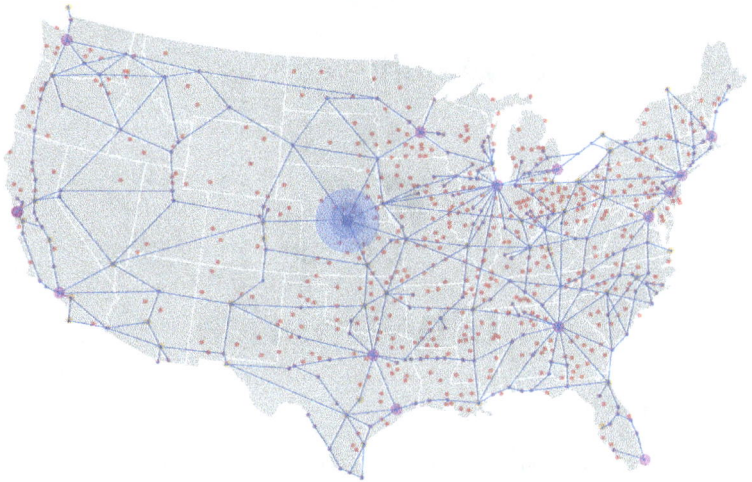

CityAmerica will be wholly owned by USA Enterprises, and therefore by the People. Every dollar in profit from CityAmerica companies will fund resident benefits and support the growth of USA Enterprises.

Leveraging best practices from other big cities, CityAmerica will feature high-density, mixed-use urban centers with abundant green space, pedestrian-only streets and plazas, and an advanced underground transportation system.

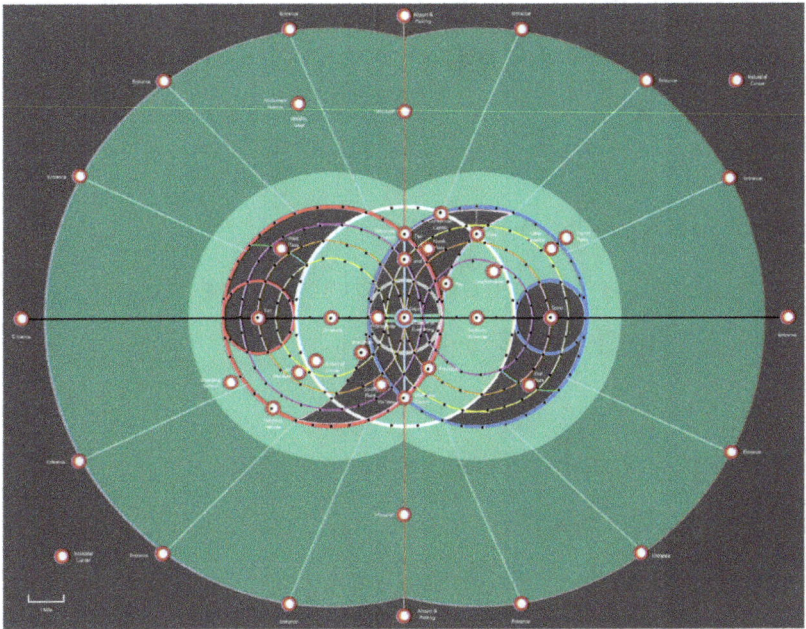

With a focus on cultivating and showcasing American ingenuity and imagination, CityAmerica will attract residents and tourists from across the country and around the world.

○
CITYPLEX

Cityplex

Cityplex, America's prototype city of the future, will be a smaller-scale proof-of-concept for CityAmerica and a template for future city development.

It'll serve as a hub for arts, culture, and innovation, and feature cutting-edge technology and sustainable design.

A living urban laboratory with a mission to find solutions to modern cities' greatest problems, Cityplex will be constructed from the ground up to pilot, showcase, and scale new technologies and social welfare programs.

♥ ⌂ ● ◆ ★

CHAPTER EIGHT:
IMPLEMENTATION & PROGRESSION

With an eye toward 2050 and beyond, we'll take a multi-stage approach to implement our vision.

Phase One
In the first phase, we'll distribute this book to people like you to raise awareness and build grassroots support for the Smart Nation plan.

We'll also launch a cultural movement, #DreamAgain, to elevate the Smart Nation ideas through art and entertainment.

#DreamAgain

Phase Two

In the second phase, we'll organize an interparty coalition to reunify our country around a common set of values, principles, and plans.

We'll also launch Public HQ, a digital public square, and equip all candidates (regardless of party affiliation) with tools and resources to campaign effectively.

Phase Three

In the third phase, we'll develop the financial infrastructure to support USA Enterprises.

Through the sale of Americoin – our new, interest-bearing currency – we'll raise capital to fund the development of the first generation of USA Enterprises.

During this phase, we'll also begin the process of modernizing our government to be leaner, more efficient, and more effective.

Phase Four

In the fourth phase, we'll create and launch USA Enterprises to begin generating profit.

In particular, USA Markets will sell and deliver all goods and services.

Phase Five

In the fifth phase, we'll cut your taxes and launch universal benefits and programs: healthcare, housing, income, and education.

During this phase, USA Works will build our transcontinental high-speed rail and autonomous vehicle thoroughfare, as well as our proof-of-concept smart city, Cityplex.

And with SpaceCo's guidance, USA Space will help construct our space infrastructure, enabling us to put a person on Mars.

Phase Six

In the sixth phase, we'll continue to scale USA Enterprises and introduce the platform to the rest of the world.

We'll complete the construction of USA Ways, our nationwide high-speed rail and autonomous vehicle superhighway network.

And we'll create CityAmerica, our nation's new economic capital.

2050 and Beyond

To stay on track, we'll update our 25-year plan every five years.

CHAPTER NINE:
CONCLUSION

You deserve a better way of life.

Smart Nation envisions a future where automation ushers in an era of efficiency and abundance, ultimately improving the quality of life for all and saving our planet.

By investing in your new benefits, we'll ensure that your needs are met and, in doing so, empower you to pursue your passions and achieve your dreams.

And leveraging automation technologies, we'll rebuild our infrastructure and transition to a sustainable economy.

We have a responsibility to future generations to create a better world than the one we inherited. As a nation of innovators and pioneers, the

United States is well-positioned to lead the charge.

It's time for change. *Radical* change.

Working together, we can build a new America – with freedom, opportunity, and justice for all – and inspire the world to reimagine our shared destiny.

—

Join the Revolution. Visit SmartNationHQ.com to learn more about how you can get involved.

Believe in America.

About Smart Nation

Smart Nation is an interparty coalition to reunify the United States of America around a common set of values, principles, and plans.

CARE • HOUSING • INCOME • EDUCATION • FREEDOM

For you. For all.

SMART NATION

www.ingramcontent.com/pod-product-compliance
Lightning Source LLC
Chambersburg PA
CBHW060513280326
41933CB00014B/2952